Tom Tit Tot

Jackanory Stories

Tom Tit Tot
and other stories

Illustrated by Jo Worth

British Broadcasting Corporation

Published by the
British Broadcasting Corporation
35 Marylebone High Street
London WIM 4AA

ISBN 0 563 12576 4

First published 1974

Printed in England by Hazell Watson & Viney Ltd,
Aylesbury, Bucks

Contents

Tom Tit Tot

Once upon a time, a long time ago, there was an old Suffolk woman who lived with her daughter. Now the daughter was very beautiful, but she was lazy and sometimes a bit stupid.

One day the old woman baked five pies. And when she took them out of the oven, she found that she'd overbaked them – the crusts were too hard to eat. So she said to her daughter: "Now, you put them there pies on the shelf and leave them there for a while until they come again."

That's an old saying – it means leaving them until the crusts get soft again.

But, the girl, she says to herself: "Well, if they'll come again, I could eat them now and it'd be all right because they'll come again and we can have them for supper."

So she set to work and ate them all, the first and the last.

She left the five dishes on the shelf and went away,

thinking that the five pies would "come again" for their supper.

That evening, the old woman said to her daughter: "Go you and get a couple of them there pies. I dare say they've come again by now, most likely."

So the daughter went to the pantry and looked. There were the five pie dishes – but there were no pies in them. "How strange," she thought, "they should have come again by now."

So she went back and said to her mother: "No, they ain't come again."

"What?" said the old woman. "Not none of 'em come again?"

"No, not none of 'em," said her daughter.

"Well, come again or not come again," said the woman, "I'll have one for my supper."

"But you can't if they haven't come," said the daughter.

"Oh, but I can – go you and bring me the softest one."

"Soft or hard," said the girl, "I ate them all, so you can't have one till they come again."

Well, then the woman realised what her daughter had done and how foolish she'd been, and she was very angry. She fetched her spinning wheel and took it into the street outside. She span and she span and as she span, she sang this song:

"My daughter ha' ate five, five pies today,
My daughter ha' ate five, five pies today."

Well, it happened to be an evening when the king was riding back to Framlingham Castle and when he passed the old woman spinning on her doorstep he heard her singing. But he couldn't make out the exact words of her song, so he stopped in front of her wheel, got off his horse, and walked up to her.

"What were you singing?" he asked.

The old woman looked up and, seeing it was the king, she didn't know what to say. She didn't want the king to think that her daughter was so silly so she sang:

"My daughter ha' spun five, five skeins today
My daughter ha' spun five, five skeins today."

"Five skeins a day! I never heard tell of anyone who could do that," said the king, and commanded the woman to bring her daughter to him.

Then he said: "See here, I want a wife – and I shall marry your daughter. But there's just one thing – for eleven months of the year, she shall have all she wants to eat and all the gowns she likes to get, and all the company she likes to keep. But on the first day of the last month, and for every other day of that month, she will have to spin five skeins every day. And if she doesn't – I'll kill her."

Well, the old woman thought this would be a grand marriage. And the thought of her daughter having to spin five skeins a day didn't really worry her. They had eleven months to work out some way of getting them spun – and she thought, like as not, the king will have forgotten about the bargain by then.

And so, the king and the girl were married.

For eleven months, the girl had all the food and drink she wanted, all the fine gowns she cared to choose, and lived like a queen. But towards the end of the eleventh month she began to worry about spinning those skeins, and neither she nor her mother had any idea how to get five skeins spun each day. But never a word did the king say about them.

However, on the last night of the month, the king collected her, and took her to a room in a tower she'd never set eyes on before. It was empty, except for a stool and a spinning wheel.

"Now my dear," he said, "this is where you'll be locked away with some flax and food and drink, and if you haven't spun five skeins by tomorrow night, off comes your head." And he left her there – locking the door behind him.

Well, of course, the girl was very frightened, for she was lazy, and had never learned to spin. And with no one to get in to help her, what should she do? She sat down on the stool and cried and cried.

All of a sudden, she heard a strange whirring noise. She looked up and there, sitting on the spinning wheel was a small black creature with a long tail.

"Where did you come from?" she asked the creature.

"Through the window," it replied. "What are you crying for?"

"What's it to you?"

"Never you mind," it said. "You tell me why you're crying."

"Won't do me any good if I do tell you."

"Aha! You don't know that!" insisted the creature and it spun its long black tail round and round.

"Well," said the girl, "I don't suppose it'll do me any good but I can't see that it'll do me any harm either." And she told the black creature the whole story about the pies and skeins and everything. The creature cocked its head on one side and listened carefully.

"Now then," it said, when she'd finished, "this is what I'll do. I'll come to this window every morning and collect the flax and return every night with five spun skeins – what do you say to that?"

Of course, the girl was delighted – this was the answer to all her problems. But she was suspicious.

"And what do you want in return?" she asked the creature.

It whirled its tail round and round, looked at her out of the corners of its eyes, and said: "I'll give you three chances each night to guess my name. If you haven't guessed it by the end of the month, you shall be mine."

The girl thought for a minute and decided that in such a long time she couldn't fail to guess the creature's name. "All right," she said. "I agree."

"Right," said the creature, and whirled its tail again. "Give me the flax and I'll be back this evening with your five skeins." And off it flew.

That evening, sure enough, the black creature flew in through the window with five skeins of spun flax over its arm.

"Here it is," it said, handing the flax to the girl. "Now then, what's my name?"

The girl had decided to go through the alphabet first of all, so she said: "Is it – Adam?"

"No, it's not," said the creature, and twirled its tail.

"Well, is it Bill?"

"No, it's not," said the creature, and twirled its tail.

"Um – is it Colin?"

"No, it's not," and it twirled its tail even faster, and away it flew.

At that moment there was a rattling at the lock of the door, and in came the king. "Well now my dear," he says, "I see you've spun your five skeins and I shan't have to have your head chopped off. You'll have more food and drink and flax tomorrow, and I'll come back at night for the five skeins."

And so, every day the girl was brought flax and food and every day the black creature took away the flax and came back with five skeins . . . and so it went on. But the girl couldn't find the creature's name. She sat there all *day* thinking, but every night she was wrong. And then it came to the last day but one.

That night, as usual, the creature flew in with the five skeins.

"Well," it said, "and what's my name?"

The girl thought and thought and thought. "Is it Nicodemus?" she asked.

"No it's not," it said.

"Is it Samuel?"

"No it's not," it said.

"Is it Zacharaiah?"

"No – it's not that either," it said.

The creature chuckled and looked at her full of malice. Then it whirled its tail round and round and said: "Only one more night to guess my name, and then you'll be mine!"

And away it flew.

The girl was really worried now, and sat down on the stool to cry. But very soon she heard footsteps along the corridor and the king came in. He looked at the five skeins and kissed the girl.

"My dear," he said, "you've proved to me that you can spin five skeins a day just as your mother said. If you spin five more tomorrow, they shall be the last you will ever have to spin. And since I reckon I won't have to kill you, I'll have supper in here tonight."

So they brought supper and a stool, and the two sat down to eat. But the girl still had to find out the creature's name. She was lost in her own thoughts, when suddenly the king began to laugh.

"Something very funny happened today when I was out hunting," he said. "In the middle of the wood I got off my horse and found an old chalk pit. And peering down I saw a strange black creature with a long tail sitting spinning away very fast, and singing. I crept up to hear and the words were:

'Nimmy, nimmy, not,
My name's Tom Tit Tot'."

Well, the girl could have jumped out of her skin for joy – but she didn't say a word.

Next night, when the creature came back with the skeins, the little red eyes gleamed and the long tail whirled round and round.

"Now then," it said, "what's my name?"

"Is it Solomon?" she asked, pretending to be afraid.

"No, it's not," it said, coming nearer to her.

"Well, is it Zebedee?"

"No! No, it's not. Now, take time woman, this is your last guess and then you're mine." And it twirled its tail so fast you could hardly see it. The girl stared at the creature, and suddenly she laughed and sang:

> *"Nimmy, nimmy, not,*
> *Your name's Tom Tit Tot!"*

The creature let out an awful shriek and flew out of the window, across the moat and into the forest. And it was never seen or heard of again.

Lod and the Giants

Long, long ago, there were giants living in Scotland. They caused a lot of trouble – they frightened children, ruined crops, knocked down houses, and generally made mischief.

One day, the King started losing his cattle – one cow after another disappeared. There was no trace of them, and although the King suspected the animals might have been taken by one of the giants, he could not prove it. His cowherd took fright and fled away, leaving no one to look after the rest of the King's animals.

About this time, a young man called Lod decided to leave home and explore the countryside. He was the son of a poor farmer and thought perhaps he could earn some money on his travels to send home.

Lod was a strong handsome lad, fearful of nothing, and he was ready to leave with only the clothes he stood up in, but his father insisted that he took with him a weapon of some sort with which he could defend himself in case of need.

"Thank you Father," said Lod, "then I would be

grateful for an iron club strong enough to protect me."

"You shall have it," said the father. He went immediately to the blacksmith, who made a club with thirty pounds weight of iron. Lod took hold of the club, raised it, and hit a rock with it. But Lod was so strong and he hit so hard that the iron broke in two.

Lod's father went back to the blacksmith and asked him to make a stronger club. The blacksmith set to work and made a club from a hundred pounds weight of iron. It was so strong that this time when Lod tried it, the iron didn't split – it just bent.

"You have been very kind and generous to me Father – do not bother to have another club made – I will make do with this one," said Lod. And he put the club across his knee and pulled and pulled it until it was back to shape again. Then he said goodbye to his parents and set off to see the world and find his fortune.

He had only travelled across country for two days when he met the King looking after his own cows – and he wasn't doing it very well, for a King is not used to such work.

"May I help you sir?" asked Lod. "My father has a few cows on his farm, and I know how to milk and feed them."

"Gladly," replied the King. "I have been looking for someone like you. I will pay you well for the work

you do – but I must warn you not to leave the cows unattended for they are disappearing one by one!"

"I will do as you ask, sir," said Lod.

So Lod settled down to look after the cows. The next day he was out in the field with them, when he heard a rumble like thunder in the distance. He looked in the bushes and through the trees, but could see nothing. The noise grew louder and the ground began to shake, then over the trees strode a great giant. As he looked down to choose a cow, he saw Lod.

"What are you doing here?" the giant said with

such a roar that the branches of the trees shook.

"Just looking after the cows," replied Lod. "I mean no harm, so please do not frighten me – just take a cow, then go away and leave me in peace."

This seemed to satisfy the giant, so he picked up the fattest cow in the herd and tied its legs together, and tried to put it on his back.

"If you promise not to hurt me," said Lod, "I will help you put the cow on your shoulders."

"I won't touch you – yet," muttered the giant under his breath.

"Bend down," said Lod, "and put your head between the cow's legs. Then I will go behind you and lift it up, and you will be able to carry it round your neck, just as the shepherds carry sheep."

The giant seemed to think this was a good idea. He bent down, but no sooner had he done so than Lod crept behind and hit the giant's head with the iron club. Then he untied the cow and hid the giant's body with leaves and bushes.

Lod went back to the King's palace that night with all the cows.

The King was surprised and pleased, but Lod didn't tell him of his adventures with the giant.

The next day, Lod took the cows out to graze in the field again. The same thing happened – Lod heard a terrible noise but this time he knew it must be a giant's footsteps so he wasn't so surprised when the giant came striding over the trees.

"Have you seen a man exactly like myself?" asked the second giant. "My twin brother has disappeared and my mother is angry."

"No, I am just here looking after these cows," said Lod.

"Oh, well, I will take one of them as a present for my mother," said the giant, and he stooped down, picked up a fat cow and tied its legs together.

Just as the day before, Lod offered to help, and again

as the giant bent down, Lod felled him with his iron club, released the cow, and covered the giant with leaves and bushes.

That night, when Lod went back to the palace, the King was overjoyed to find he hadn't lost any cows. The King wanted to know how he had managed it but Lod would not explain.

Next day, Lod took the cows to graze again, thinking that there could be no more giants left. But he was wrong.

Before long, a terrible wind blew up and over the trees, puffing and blowing, came a terrible hag. Her hair was grey and tangled, her clothes were in tatters, and her nails were sharp and long. She pointed one of them at Lod.

"You have killed my two sons," she shouted. "Now I have come to get my revenge."

Then she bent down to take up Lod, but as she put one hand round his waist, he grabbed her at the knee and pulled hard. She lost her balance and fell to the ground.

Lod thought that her weight would squeeze the life out of him, but he managed somehow to struggle free. Then he pulled her shawl over her head so that she couldn't see.

By the time she had untangled herself, Lod had picked up his iron club. Every time the hag tried to get up, he swung the club very hard near her head. "If you stop doing that I will give you my treasure," she screamed.

"What treasure, and where is it?" called Lod, swinging the club faster and faster.

"Gold and silver and jewels that my sons have stolen for me," cried the Hag. "Now stop tormenting me."

"Only when you have told me where this treasure is hidden," said Lod, and he swung the club so near that it made the hag cry in fear.

"It's hidden in the cave by the oak tree over there. *Now* stop tormenting me," she pleaded.

"I will indeed. I will put you out of your misery, and also stop you hurting my kind of people," said Lod. And with that he swung the club so that it felled the hag with one blow. He covered her like her sons with leaves and bushes, then he took the cows home.

But when he got to the palace the King didn't come and see him as usual. Instead he found all the people standing in small groups, some crying and some talking quietly. But all were upset about the terrible fate of the King's daughter.

While Lod had been walking back with the herd of cows, a terrible Giant-with-three-heads had arrived at the Palace. He had asked for the King's daughter to be delivered to him in his cave by the oak tree in the grazing field by sunrise the next day. If the Princess didn't come, then the Giant-with-three-heads would take his revenge by killing everyone in the country.

Now Lod was very angry when he heard this, for this giant must live in the cave where the hag had kept her treasures. The hag had played a trick on him, for how could Lod get out the gold and silver and jewels with such a terrible giant there? But most of all, Lod was upset because he had loved the Princess since the first moment he had set eyes on her.

The King had sadly decided it was his duty to give his daughter to the giant in order to save the lives of all his people. The Princess was to be sent to the giant very early the next day.

As she was leaving, the palace cook – who was really a scoundrel and out for all he could get – asked the

King if he could escort the Princess.

"And when I get to the cave I will try to kill the giant. If I do, may I have a reward?"

The King didn't like the man, but anything was worth trying to save his daughter. So he said, "Whoever kills the giant shall marry my daughter."

The cook and the Princess set off for the cave. When Lod heard, he guessed what terrible danger the Princess was in, and followed them with his iron club.

He found the Princess waiting outside the cave, shivering and trembling – waiting for the giant to seize her and take her inside for ever.

The cook was hiding behind a tree, for he was a great coward, and not only that, but a great deceiver.

When the Princess saw Lod she called to him, "Why have you come? Surely you do not want to be killed by the giant?"

"I have come to rescue you – I am used to such things as giants and I think I can deal with him."

The Giant-with-three-heads heard this and gave a great roar. A huge, ugly monster blundered from the cave and as he came out of the darkness into the bright light the sun blinded his six eyes. Quick as a flash Lod told the Princess to hide, and at the same time he brandished his club and hit the giant at the knee. It caught the giant off his balance, and he fell down.

Lod raced round and with three swipes hit each of the giant's heads. It was the end of the giant. It was almost the end of Lod too, for he had hit so hard that on the third blow he fell to the ground and badly cut his wrist on a sharp stone.

Seeing this the Princess ran over, tore off the bottom of her petticoat and tied it tightly round Lod's wound. Before long the bleeding stopped and Lod's life was saved. The Princess told him to rest for a while.

The cook had been watching all this and when he

saw Lod was asleep he seized the boot from the dead giant, grasped the Princess and hurried with them back to the palace.

"Sire," he said to the King, "I have slain the giant and I have brought you his boot to prove it. Now may I marry your daughter?" The King felt he must keep his promise. The Princess wanted to tell him of the trick that had been played by the cook; but she had nothing to prove the truth.

The wedding arrangements were made – the marriage was to take place the same evening. Everyone at the palace was invited.

As soon as Lod recovered he searched for the Princess. When he couldn't find her in either the cave or the field he went hurrying back to the palace.

He arrived as the King was greeting the wedding guests. They lined up, the men bowed and the women curtsied. When he had greeted them all, the King exclaimed, "There is still one of my loyal subjects missing – my cowherd, where is he?" As soon as he said this, Lod entered.

"Father," cried the Princess. "*This* is the man who really rescued me by killing the giant. And Father, I can prove it." She rushed over to Lod and gently pulled him towards the King. "Look, Father," she said, "his wrist was slashed as he killed the giant. I bandaged it with cloth from my petticoat." She raised the bottom of her wedding dress to reveal the torn garment. The delicate embroidery on it matched the blood-stained cloth on Lod's arm.

The Princess turned to Lod. "I wouldn't change my petticoat in case you came back in time."

"In time?" asked Lod, still dazed.

"In time," the Princess explained, "to stop me having to marry the cook – for I really want to marry you."

Nobody noticed the cook creeping out of the palace, and nobody minded that he was never seen again.

Lod told the King of all his adventures with the giants, and how the hag had left him her fortune.

The King went to the field to see where the giants lay, and then appointed a new cow-herd for his cattle.

Lod collected the gold and silver and jewels and bought his parents a new farm with fine cattle and rich pasture land.

Then he returned, built a magnificent palace, and with the King's consent married the Princess. And then, they lived happily ever after!

Master of all Masters

Once upon a time there was a very crotchety old man. He lived alone except for one servant who did all the work of the house. But none of his servants ever stayed more than a week!

They would arrive on a Monday morning. And the old man would say: "Monday you work. Tuesday you work. Wednesday and Thursday and Friday you work. Saturday you work, and Sunday you work. And then, in the evening, if I'm satisfied, I'll give you your wages."

But the old man never had to pay any wages. For every Sunday, there'd be a shouting and screaming from inside the house. The front door would burst open, the servant would rush out in tears, and the old man would throw her baggage out after her. And the old man hadn't paid her any wages!

Then one Monday morning he opened his door to find a smiling country girl standing on his doorstep.

"My name's Bridie O'Flanagan," said she. "And I've come to be your servant. Monday I'll work.

Tuesday I'll work. Wednesday and Thursday and Friday I'll work. Saturday I'll work and Sunday I'll work. And if you don't pay me my wages on Sunday night, my name's not Bridie O'Flanagan!"

And in she stepped and on with her apron. In no time at all the house was clean and bright as a new pin. Bridie did everything she could think of to please her master, and they got on fine together all the week.

But then came Sunday, and from the moment he got out of bed the old man grumbled. He brought dirt in from the garden all over Bridie's newly-washed floor. When she brought his Sunday roast, he said he wanted fish. When she brought him fruit, he demanded cheese. But Bridie O'Flanagan never batted an eyelid, and went about her work smiling as usual. The old man grew crosser and crosser.

After supper he called Bridie to his room and said: "Monday you worked. Tuesday you worked. Wednesday and Thursday and Friday you worked. Saturday you worked, and Sunday you worked. But I'm not satisfied, oh no! For one thing, what d'you call me?"

"Why," said Bridie, "I call you Master or Mister, or whatever you will, sir."

"No," cried the old man, "you must call me 'Master of all Masters', do you hear?"

"I hear," said Bridie. And she started to go away.

"Wait a moment," said the old man, pointing to his

trousers, "what d'you call these?"

"Why, trousers or breeches or whatever you will, sir."

"No, no!" said the old man. "They're 'squibs and crackers', that's what they are!"

"Very well sir," said Bridie, and she bobbed him a curtsy.

"And what's that?" demanded the old man, pointing to his bed.

"Your bed or your couch or whatever you will, sir," said Bridie.

"That's my barnacle!" said the old man. "Don't you forget it!"

"I won't," said Bridie. And she called to the cat who was hiding under the bed: "Puss, puss, puss! What are you doing under there?"

"That's not a puss!" shouted the old man. "That's my white-faced Simminy! Get out of here!" and he shooed the creature away very angrily.

"Oh, I daresay white-faced Simminy will be happier in the garden," said Bridie pleasantly. "But what about you, Master of all Masters? Are you cold, shall I light the fire?"

"Fire? Fire? What d'you mean, fire? Light the hot cockalorum!"

"Hot cockalorum? Oh? Light the hot cockalorum," said Bridie. "Fancy that now!"

And she soon had a bright fire blazing in the hearth.

Well, even after that, the old man wasn't satisfied. He went into the garden and called to Bridie to bring him a drink.

"Will a glass of water do?" she asked.

"What did you call it?" snapped the old man.

"Why, water or wet or whatever you will, sir," said Bridie.

"Pondolorum, that's what I will!" cried the old man. "Pondolorum, that's what it is." And as Bridie O'Flanagan hurried back into the house he shouted after her angrily: "What d'you call that, eh?" pointing towards the house.

"House or home or whatever you will, sir," called Bridie.

"No, no, no!" shrieked the old man. "That's my high top o' mountain! High top o'mountain, and don't you forget it!"

That very night, when the old man was fast asleep in bed, Bridie O'Flanagan rushed into his room. And she shook him till he woke in a fright. Then: "Master of all Masters," said she, "get out of your barnacle, put on your squibs and crackers, white-faced Simminy has got a spot of hot cockalorum on her tail and unless you put some pondolorum on mighty quick high top o'mountain will be all on hot cockalorum!"

And that was the last time that old man wanted to be called Master of all Masters.

Thomas the Rhymer

There was once a man called Thomas Learmont, who lived in Ercildoune, a little village which lay beneath the Eildon hills in the Scottish border country. The land there is rich and green, and like most of the villagers, Thomas was a farmer. He had a few cows and a few sheep, and he lived in a small cottage not far from the River Tweed. He was a popular man in the village, for if he told a few white lies now and again and boasted about his cattle, well, so did everyone else. And he was a cheerful fellow, and could play the lute more sweetly than anyone else in the valley.

Thomas often wandered off to the woods by himself to play his lute. He used to lie on a mossy bank, and play softly to himself for hours and hours. Villagers from Ercildoune strolling in the woods would stop and listen to the melody.

Then one day something strange happened to Thomas. Sitting alone in the woods, he began to feel very drowsy and soon fell asleep. He was wakened by the sound of bells coming through the trees. He shook

his head. "I must still be dreaming," he said to himself, and closed his eyes.

But there was the sound again – nearer this time. It was definitely bells; hundreds of tiny, tinkling bells. Thomas stood up and peered through the trees, and what he saw there made him gasp in amazement.

Coming toward him was a milk-white horse – its mane hung with hundreds of tiny silver bells. They tinkled as the horse tossed its head from side to side.

But it was the rider who held Thomas spellbound. For on the horse's back was the most beautiful lady Thomas had ever seen. Her long hair fell like a golden waterfall round her shoulders, her skin was white as snow and her eyes black as midnight. She wore a bright green dress and a long green velvet cloak.

When the lovely rider reached Thomas, she smiled and held out her hand to him. In a daze, Thomas helped her off the horse, then fell on his knees before her.

"Don't be afraid, Thomas," said she. "I am the Queen of Elfland. I heard your music from far away and I had to come and listen – please won't you play for me again?"

Thomas took up his lute and played more beautifully than he had ever played before.

When he had finished the Elfin Queen said: "Thomas, what can I give you, to reward you for your wonderful playing?"

Thomas seized both the Queen's hands and fell on his knees before her again. "Give me just one kiss, fair Queen," he begged, "and I will be happy for the rest of my life.

"If I kiss you, Thomas," said the Elf Queen, "you will fall under my spell, and will have to come back to Elfland with me for seven years."

"What are seven years compared with the joy of a kiss?" cried Thomas.

He rose from his knees, drew the lovely Elf Queen towards him, and kissed her. As he stepped back and looked into her eyes, he knew he was caught in her spell, and would have to follow wherever she led.

The Elf Queen mounted her horse again and Thomas found himself jumping up behind her. Then they sped back through the woods. The great white horse galloped so fast Thomas thought they must be flying. Through the trees they went, then over heather, over broad rivers, bushes and rocks, and all the time the sky got darker and darker.

When at last the horse came to a halt Thomas knew he was in a completely strange country. He couldn't see the Eildon Hills any more, and the sky was blacker than he could ever remember it.

"Don't be afraid, Thomas," said the Queen, "we are nearly in Elfland – but before we go any further I want you to promise me something. While you are in my country you must not speak; for seven years you will have to stay silent and then you can return to Ercil-doune. But if you break your promise and speak even one word, you will be doomed to spend the rest of your life in a dark terrible place, and will never be able to get back home."

This seemed very harsh to Thomas. He knew how difficult it is not to speak for one day, let alone seven years. Thomas wasn't sure he could keep such a promise.

"If I'm hungry, what way shall I ask for food, and if I'm thirsty, what way shall I ask for water?" he asked.

"Don't worry," replied the Queen. "In Elfland you will have all you need without ever having to ask."

"Then I will make the promise. I swear I won't speak one word for seven years," said Thomas.

The Queen smiled. "You will never regret your

promise," said she. Then she gently shook the reins and the white horse set off again.

Soon the countryside changed, and they were flying over heather all bright in the sunlight. Thomas heard the sound of trumpets as they approached two huge golden gates. The gates swung open when the Queen's horse reached them, and Thomas found himself in the most beautful country he had ever seen.

As soon as Thomas saw Elfland, he knew that he would never regret his promise. It was a place where there were no wars. No one ever told a lie or cheated, and everyone was content. Thomas lived there happily and during those seven years he never spoke a word. He served the Queen and watched and listened, and so he learned many things and grew a much wiser man than he was before. Those seven years in Elfland were the happiest he had ever known.

When the day came for Thomas to leave, the Queen herself led him outside the golden gates.

"You can break your silence now, Thomas," she said, "but I want to reward you for keeping your promise, and for serving me so well."

She took an apple from a tree beside the gates and held it out to Thomas. "This is a magic apple," she said. "If you eat it your tongue will never tell a lie."

Thomas was uncertain. "I would like to tell the truth all the time," he said, "but at times I have to tell a few white lies, to get a good price for my cattle, or to flatter a lady who isn't very beautiful. People don't always like it if you tell them the truth."

"I promise that if you eat this apple it won't get you into trouble, but bring you great fame and happiness," the Queen said.

As Thomas was biting into the apple she added:

"Before you go there is just one more promise I want you to make."

"What's that?" asked Thomas, for he was still very anxious to please the Queen.

"One day I shall need you back in Elfland," said the Queen, "and I want you to promise that when that day comes you will return to me immediately."

"But how shall I know when you need me?" asked Thomas.

"I will send two messengers," said the Queen, "and as soon as you see them, you will know that they come from Elfland. They will guide you back to me."

Thomas was glad to be going back to Ercildoune, but he knew he would miss the Queen and never be truly happy until he saw her again, so he eagerly made his promise.

The Queen smiled at Thomas and her great black eyes gazed into his. Then the golden gates of Elfland seemed to melt away and he began to feel dizzy. A white mist fell all around him and he sank to the ground in a deep sleep.

Thomas woke up on the bank where he had been lying exactly seven years before.

When he looked up he could see the blue hills and he knew that he was in his own country again. His lute was still in his hands and everything seemed so much the same he began to wonder if he had dreamt about his years in Elfland. So he set off to Ercildoune to find out if he really had been away for seven years. He didn't have to wait long. The first person he saw was a neighbour. The poor man gave a shriek and fell down in a dead faint. He thought Thomas had died and come back as a ghost. The same thing happened with the next two people Thomas met, and by the time he had reached the centre of the village a whole crowd had gathered on the green, waiting to see Thomas Learmont's ghost.

Thomas soon showed them he was no ghost, and told the villagers the whole story. To his surprise, he found that he couldn't bring himself to tell even one tiny white lie. And although his story was so strange, Thomas's eyes looked so honest and straightforward, the villagers knew he couldn't be lying.

Only one thing did Thomas never speak about – his promise to return to Fairyland when the Queen's messengers called for him.

Not many things had changed while Thomas had been away for seven years. He found his cottage roof needed repairing, and his neighbours looked a bit older, but on the whole the village and the countryside looked the same. It was Thomas who was different – he looked the same, but he had become much wiser.

He became more popular than ever. People came

from all over the border to hear his wonderful story, and even dukes and earls sent for him to ask his advice. Thomas found that he could always answer their questions and, what was more, whatever he said came true. For this the rich earls paid him very well.

But there was something odd about Thomas's answers: they were nearly always in rhyme. For instance when Haig, the Laird of Bemersyde, was getting old he asked Thomas if a Haig would always be laird. Now Haig already had twelve daughters, and it didn't seem likely that he would ever have a son to

succeed him. But Thomas replied:

"Betide, betide, what'eer betide
A Haig shall be Haig of Bemersyde"

and sure enough in a few months Haig's wife had a son, who became laird when his father died. Soon all Scotland had heard about Thomas, and he became known as Thomas the Rhymer. With the money he earned he built a grand castle in Ercildoune and every year he gave a great banquet.

Everyone in the village was invited. A huge meal was provided and as much ale as anyone could want.

After the feast everyone danced to the music of the pipes. But in the middle of all this gaiety, Thomas would sit alone with a faraway look in his eyes. No one knew that he was still dreaming of the Elfin Queen.

Then, one cold mid-winter, Thomas gave a banquet larger and more wonderful than ever before. When everyone had eaten and danced as much as they could, Thomas took up his old lute and began to play. A hush fell on the crowd and they all gathered round Thomas to hear his wonderful playing.

Suddenly there was a loud knocking on the door and a servant burst in. His eyes were wild with fear and he had run so fast his chest was heaving. When he could get enough breath to speak he gasped out: "Oh, sir – I have seen the most amazing thing. Two deer have come out of the forest and into the village – they are walking straight up to this castle – nothing seems to stop them. It seems as if they know exactly where they are going. But there is something strange about these deer, sir, they are both milk-white and have silver horns. And I'm afraid."

The villagers gasped – such a thing had never been heard of before. They were afraid it was a sign that something terrible was about to happen.

"What does it mean?" they cried.

But Thomas didn't reply – he just walked slowly to the open door. The crowd parted to let him through, then followed him outside. There, coming up the moonlit path, were the two strange deer. They were as white as the snow, and their silver horns glistened in the moonlight. The crowd shrank back in terror, but Thomas's face shone with happiness. He knew that at last the Elfin Queen wanted him to return to her. The milk-white deer were the messengers the Queen had promised she would send to guide him back to Elfland.

When the deer saw Thomas coming toward them, they stopped and waited for him. Then they turned back to the forest and, with Thomas between them, they walked slowly out of the village.

Thomas the Rhymer was never seen again.

Dick Whittington

In the reign of King Edward III in a village in Gloucestershire lived a poor boy called Dick Whittington. His father and mother had died when he was young, so he was all alone in the world.

Sometimes he worked in the fields and earned himself a crust of bread to eat. The farmers were kind, but they were poor too, and Dick often went hungry.

One day some travellers came to the village and Dick overheard them talking about the great city of London where there was singing and dancing all day long and "the streets were paved with gold". Dick had never seen a city, so he made up his mind to go to London and see the golden streets for himself.

He took his stick, and some bread and cheese wrapped up in a handkerchief, and started on the walk to London. He walked and he walked through villages and towns and farms, and over hills and across bridges following the road to London. After a while he could walk no further, and he sat down by the side of the road to rest. A wagon drawn by eight horses came along, and he asked

the wagoner if he were going to London.

"Indeed I am," said the wagoner, "and you may ride beside me if you wish."

So Dick jumped up on the wagon, and rode the rest of the way to London. The wagoner put him down by London bridge, and Dick went through the streets thinking at any moment he'd find those that were paved with gold. But all he saw were people and houses, and all he heard were pedlars shouting their wares and the noise of cart wheels over the rough streets. There was no gold to be seen. At last it grew dark, and Dick sat down in a doorway and cried himself to sleep.

He woke in the morning to find he had slept in the entrance to a fine house. The cook was busy cleaning the kitchen, and she threw a bucket of dirty water over Dick, shouting at him to be off before the master, Mr Fitzwarren, found him. But just then Mr Fitzwarren himself came out.

"Why don't you go to work, my lad, instead of lying there like an idle fellow?" he asked.

"Indeed I would, sir," said Dick. "I would work for you sir, if you would only let me." Dick tried to stand, but he was faint for lack of food. Mr Fitzwarren ordered that he be taken into the house for a good dinner, and that work be found for him in the kitchen.

So Dick was set to help out in the kitchen. He would have been very happy there but for the bad-tempered cook. She shouted at him all day long, and beat him with a broom when anything went wrong. Still, Dick had food to eat and a house to live in, and Mr Fitzwarren's daughter Alice was always kind to him. And now and again he was given a penny for his labours.

Yet one thing made him very miserable. He slept at the top of the house in a little attic under the roof, and the room was infested with rats and mice. They came from the holes in the floor and ran about the room all night, sometimes even climbing onto his bed. So one day he took a penny and went into the city and bought himself a cat.

He kept her hidden in his room, and always remembered to take her some scraps from his own dinner. Very soon the cat had got rid of all the rats and mice, and Dick was able to sleep soundly, with the cat curled

up on the foot of the bed.

Now Mr Fitzwarren was a merchant who owned several trading ships. The ships took goods from London far across the seas, where the captain would exchange the cargo for gold or jewels or other valuables. And it was the custom in Mr Fitzwarren's house that when the ship was about to sail, each of the servants was asked if he had anything to send on the trading ship. Mr Fitzwarren was a generous man, and liked his household to share in his good fortune.

When it came to Dick's turn, he did not come to his master like the other servants, for he had nothing to send. Alice offered to send something of hers in Dick's name, but her father said that it must be Dick's very own.

"Sir, I have nothing to send on your ship," said Dick, "for I have nothing of my own in this world, except my cat which I bought for a penny."

"Then bring the cat, my lad," said Mr Fitzwarren, "and we'll send her on the ship."

Dick parted with his cat sadly, for he had grown very fond of her. He would be lonely in his attic now, and without Puss the rats and mice would soon return.

The other servants teased him for having sent his cat on the ship, and the cook, who was jealous of his friendship with Alice, made his life even more miserable.

At last Dick could bear it no longer. Early one morning, taking his stick and a crust in his handkerchief as before, he ran away. He got as far as Highgate Hill, a few miles from the city, and there he sat down on a stone and looked at London far below. Then he heard the sound of the bells of Bow church ringing out. And they seemed to say:

"Turn again Whittington,
Thou worthy citizen,
Lord Mayor of London,
And feast with the King."

"I wonder," thought Dick. "To be Lord Mayor of London would be splendid indeed. But it could never happen if I run away now. I will go back and try again."

So Dick went back, and was lucky enough to creep into the house before anyone had even noticed his absence.

Now the merchant ship that Mr Fitzwarren had sent to far countries had been gone some long time, when it ran into a storm and was blown by high winds to the Barbary coast of Africa. When the King of Barbary heard that a ship from London had arrived, he sent for the captain and crew and invited them to a feast. While they were eating and drinking, the King told them of a plague that had attacked his kingdom. Everywhere, in towns and villages, and even in the Royal Palace itself, there were swarms of rats and mice. They were destroying all the grain, and soon there would be nothing left.

"I would give half the treasure in my kingdom to be rid of these vermin," said he.

At that the captain remembered Dick Whittington's cat, and told the King and the royal court of Barbary that he had on board his ship an animal that would soon put an end to rats and mice.

"Bring this creature to me," said the King. "If she will do as you say, I will load your ship with gold and jewels in exchange."

The shrewd captain pretended he did not want to part with the cat. "She is of great value on the ship," said he, "for she protects my cargo against vermin. But since it is Your Majesty who asks, I will fetch her for you."

Away went the captain to the ship, and returned with

the cat in his arms. He was just in time to find the table full of rats, which had swarmed in to feast on the remains of the meal. The cat leapt from him, and in a few minutes the table was cleared of vermin. Most of the rats had been killed, the remainder had fled.

Then the captain tried to present the cat to the Queen, who at first was afraid to touch such a fierce creature. But then he stroked the cat, which purred, and soon Puss was at rest on the Queen's lap, playing with her hand and purring softly.

The King was delighted to find such a clever animal, and when he discovered after a few days that the palace was no longer over-run with the pests, he sent for the captain and gave him a vast store of gold, silver, and rich jewels. Then the captain set sail for home.

The journey took a year or more, and when the news came that the ship had at last arrived home, Dick was still working in the kitchen. Mr Fitzwarren sent for him at once.

"Mr Whittington," said he, "your cat has been sold to the King of Barbary for more riches than I possess in the world. I am very happy for you, and trust you will use your money wisely."

Dick was overjoyed, and being a kind young man he shared his treasure with the captain and the crew, and everyone in the house – even the bad-tempered cook. With his face washed, and dressed in new clothes, he went to his master and asked if he might marry Alice Fitzwarren.

A day for the wedding was soon fixed. All the richest merchants of London attended, and then were entertained to a great feast.

Afterwards, Dick Whittington and his lady lived in great splendour, and were very happy. He was Lord Mayor of London three times, and was knighted by Henry V. And one day he did entertain the King to a magnificent feast.

So the prophecy of Bow bells came true: but Dick Whittington never forgot his days as a poor boy, and did use his money wisely, to found schools and hospitals and to help the poor. Nor did he ever forget his cat, which had helped him make his fortune.

Turn again Whittington,
Thou worthy citizen,
Lord Mayor of London,
And feast with the king.

The Three Soldiers

There were once three soldiers who got separated from their regiment. When they heard they were to leave the town where they had been stationed for some months, they went to say goodbye to their friends. But they stayed too long, and when they returned to camp, the rest of the regiment had gone.

So they set out at once, hoping to catch them up. They walked and they walked and they walked until it got dark. Then, far away in the distance, they saw a light. When they drew near, they found it shone from a small house.

The house door was open, the floor swept and a good fire burning. The three soldiers, whose names were Colin, Patrick and John, sat round the fire warming themselves. Then John saw a light under an inner door, and in the other room there was a table laid with every kind of food. He started eating, although the others tried to stop him.

"It's not our food," they said. But he went on eating, and in the end Colin and Patrick joined him.

Then they saw there were three beds in the room, so the soldiers lay down. Before they went to sleep, three red-headed girls came into the room, and cleared the table. They left it spread with food for the next morning and went away.

Next day Colin, who was a sergeant, said they must move on to try and find the regiment, but John said *he* would not move so long as food and rest were so easy to get. They argued until supper-time, and after it till bed-time, and again the three girls came, and went leaving the table as full of food as before.

The next day was the same, and they argued the same way, and ate the same way, and the three girls came to them again. But in the morning the eldest girl gave Colin a purse.

"It is a most special purse," she said, "for every time you open it, it will be full of silver and gold."

The second red-haired girl gave Patrick, who was a corporal, a cloth. "It is a most special cloth," she said, "for every time you spread it, it will be covered with every kind of food."

The third girl gave John, the soldier, a whistle.

"It is a most special whistle," she said, "for every time you blow it you will find yourself in the middle of the army."

Then the girls left the cottage and went away.

"I can't leave it like this," said John, "I must find out who they are."

So he followed them, and when they saw him, they turned to him, weeping.

"What is the matter?" he asked.

"Much is the matter," they replied. "We are under a spell, but if we could have served you for three nights, and you had not followed us, then we would have been free."

"Is there any other way?" asked John.

"There is another way. At the end of the house there is a tree, if you come back after a year and a day, and pull it up, we shall be free."

John went back to tell the others what had happened, and then they decided to go back to the town. They knew they would never catch up with the regiment now. When they got to the town John said: "I shall go and see the King's daughter!"

"You'd better not," the others said, but he went all the same, and when he got there he knocked on the door and was taken to see the King's daughter.

"What is your business?" she asked.

"I have a whistle, a most special whistle, and when

I blow it, it will take me straight away into the middle of the army."

The King's daughter begged and pleaded and wheedled, so in the end he gave her the whistle, then she drove him downstairs and shut the door on him.

He went back to the others and asked Colin to lend him the purse. When he'd got it he went back to the King's daughter and said: "I have a purse, a most special purse, when I open it, it is full of gold and silver."

The King's daughter begged and pleaded and wheedled, so in the end he gave her the purse, then she drove him downstairs and shut the door on him.

Next John went to Patrick and asked for the loan of the cloth. When he'd got it, he went back to the King's daughter and said: "I have a cloth, a most special cloth, each time I spread it, it is covered with every kind of food."

"Let me see it," said the King's daughter.

So John spread it out, but there was one corner which would not lie flat. He asked the King's daughter to stand on it, and he stood on another corner. But the cloth was magic, and the next thing they knew they were on a beautiful island in the middle of the deep, wide sea. They wandered about the island until they were tired and then lay down to rest. The soldier slept, but the King's daughter stayed awake so that she could escape from him. She took the cloth and used its magic

to take her back to her father's house.

When the soldier woke up he was alone. The cloth had gone, and he had no food. But on the island he found two apple trees, one with red apples and one with green apples. When he ate the red apples, deer's horns grew on his head. When he ate the green apples, the horns fell off, and he was as before.

So he gathered the apples into two bags, one of red apples and one of green. Then he walked on the shore until he saw a ship come by. He waved and shouted, and when they saw him, they took him on board. The captain led him to the cabin for a meal and he left the bags on the deck. The sailors opened the bags to find out what was inside. They saw the red apples and ate them, and at once they all had deer's horns growing on their heads. They began to quarrel and fight. When the captain saw what had happened he was very angry. "You wicked man, what have you done to my sailors?" he shouted.

"Your sailors should not have stolen from my sacks," said John. "But what will you give me, if I take the horns away?" The captain was frightened by this strange man. "I will give you my ship and the cargo when we reach port," he said.

The cargo was gold, so John was well pleased. He gave the sailors green apples to eat and the horns disappeared.

As soon as they reached the port, which was the town where the King's daughter lived, John went off to visit her. He dressed in rags and pretended to be an apple-seller. "Apples for sale!" he called under the palace window. The King's daughter leaned out and ordered a pound, but he sent her one to try – a red one.

She ate it, and at once deer's horns grew on her head.

The King, her father, was furious. He announced that if anyone could cure his daughter, he should have gold and silver and the Princess as his bride.

Men came from far and wide but they could not cure her. Then John came to the Palace, and said he could do the job. He went to the Princess's room carrying a great book. He pretended to read it and be very wise and no one knew he couldn't read a word. After a while he looked up and said: "Did you at any time wheedle a whistle from a poor soldier, a most special whistle?"

"I did."

"If that special whistle is not found, I cannot cure you."

"It is found," she said and gave it to him.

Then he gave her a piece of green apple and a piece of the deer's horns fell from her head.

"I can't do more today," he said, "but I will come back tomorrow."

The next day John went to the Princess and looked at the book and said: "Did you at any time wheedle a purse from a poor soldier, a most special purse?"

"I did."

"If that special purse is not found, I cannot cure you."

"It is found," she said and gave him the purse. He gave her another piece of green apple and another piece of the deer's horns fell from her head.

The next day he went to the Princess for the third time. He stared for a long time at his book and said: "Did you ever wheedle a cloth from a poor soldier, a most special cloth?"

"I did."

"If that special cloth is not found, I cannot finish curing you."

"It is found," she said and gave him the cloth. Then he gave her a whole apple, and at once what was left of the deer's horns disappeared.

The King offered John the reward he had promised. He took the gold and silver but refused the Princess as a bride.

Instead he went to find his friends Colin and Patrick. At first they did not know him. But he said: "Do you remember the house where we stayed, and the promise we made to the three girls that we would return in a year and a day?" Then they recognised him.

"It is past that time," they said.

"No," he said, "tomorrow night is the night!"

Then he gave them the purse and the cloth while he kept the whistle.

The next night the three soldiers rode to the house and caught hold of the tree. It came up at the first pull, and there were the three beautiful red-haired girls, free from the spell.

Colin, Patrick and John rode back to the town with the girls riding pillion behind them.

Next day, they were married, and all six lived happily ever after.

Tom Thumb

In the days when King Arthur ruled the land, there lived a farmer and his wife who were very happy but for one thing. They had a neat cottage and a big garden, but they had no child to care for.

One day the farmer's wife was sitting sewing outside the cottage. She was thinking how lonely she was without a baby to rock in the wooden cradle on the hearth, and she said out loud: "Oh, I do wish I had a baby son! I wouldn't mind even if he were no bigger than my husband's thumb."

Now it happened that Merlin, the King's magician, was passing by when she said this. He thought to himself: "Well, why not? Why shouldn't the farmer's wife have a son no bigger than her husband's thumb?" So before he went on he said a few spells and did some magic, and by and by, a tiny boy was born. And because he was no bigger than a thumb they called him Tom Thumb.

The farmer's wife was delighted and nursed her baby and fed him and looked after him, but although he got

older like ordinary children do, he never grew any bigger than his father's thumb.

Now, Tom Thumb was just like ordinary boys – he liked playing games and singing songs and being naughty – and like other boys he was always getting into trouble. But because he was so small his troubles were different from other boys.

One day Tom's mother was making a batter pudding. Tom was anxious to see what was happening, so he climbed up the side of the bowl until he was standing right on the very edge, and he leaned further and further over until he suddenly overbalanced and fell right in – *splash* – all among the flour and eggs. His mother didn't see him fall, and she finished stirring the mixture, tied it up in a pudding cloth, and put it into a pot to boil.

Tom Thumb couldn't call out because his mouth was full of pudding mixture, but he kicked and struggled and squirmed so much that the pudding began to bounce about in the pot. When Tom's mother saw it she thought it was bewitched.

"Someone's put a spell on that pudding," she said, "I'm not leaving it in here," and she picked up the pot and ran out with it as fast as she could and threw it over the hedge at the bottom of the garden. When the pudding landed on the other side of the hedge it dropped thump on to the ground. The cloth split open and poor Tom was able to scramble out. He was all covered in pudding mixture, of course, and looked a terrible mess. He crept through the hedge and walked back to the garden, and when his mother saw him she was very cross.

She washed him in a teacup of warm water, and said: "There, you see, Tom Thumb, you mustn't be so careless. You're so small it's very easy for things to happen to you."

"I'm sorry, Mother. I will be more careful," said Tom.

And for a while he was. But one day when he was walking in the fields he tripped over a grass stalk, and while he was lying on the ground with his heels in the air getting his breath back, a huge black bird swooped down and snatched him up in its beak. It was a raven.

The raven thought Tom Thumb was something good

to eat and flew off with him, over woods and fields a long, long way until he was over the sea.

Then he got tired of carrying Tom Thumb, who was quite heavy for a bird – so he dropped him. Down fell Tom, down, down, down, straight into the sea with a splash! Just at that moment along came a big fish, looking for something to eat. There was Tom Thumb floating right in front of its nose, so it swallowed him up in one big gulp.

That might have been the end of Tom Thumb! But later that day the fish was caught and taken to the palace for King Arthur to have for his supper. When the royal cook opened the fish to clean it, out jumped Tom Thumb. He was a bit bad-tempered after being in the fish's tummy all day, but none the worse for all that!

The cook was very surprised. "What's this?" he said. "A boy no bigger than a person's thumb! We'd better take him to the king." So he did.

Tom Thumb stood on the king's knee so that the king could talk to him without having to bend down too much.

"Who are you?" said the king.

"Please, Your Majesty, my name's Tom Thumb," said Tom.

"And where have you come from, Tom Thumb?"

"I have been carried through the air and through the sea, Your Majesty, all the way to your court. And now that I am here perhaps I can serve you?" Tom Thumb bowed very low and the king was delighted.

"What can you do to serve me, Tom Thumb?"

"I can dance and sing, and make Your Majesty laugh," said Tom, and he started to dance.

The king laughed and picked him up. "Very well, Tom Thumb, you may stay at my court and make me laugh."

So Tom Thumb stayed at the king's court and became a great favourite. When the king went out riding Tom went with him.

The king was very pleased with his little friend and wanted to make him a present, so as his clothes were very battered after all his adventures, he ordered a new set to be made. When the clothes were ready and

Tom Thumb was dressed in them, he looked very fine. Then the king made Tom Thumb a knight – which is a great honour for anyone – so that he became *Sir* Thomas Thumb. A knight must have a horse, so he gave him a spanking white mouse to ride.

"There, Sir Thomas," said the king. "Now you are really one of my knights."

And Tom Thumb bowed low. "Thank you, Your Majesty," he said. The courtiers made up a song about the new knight and his fine new clothes.

Of butterflies' wings his shirt was made,
His boots of chicken's hide.

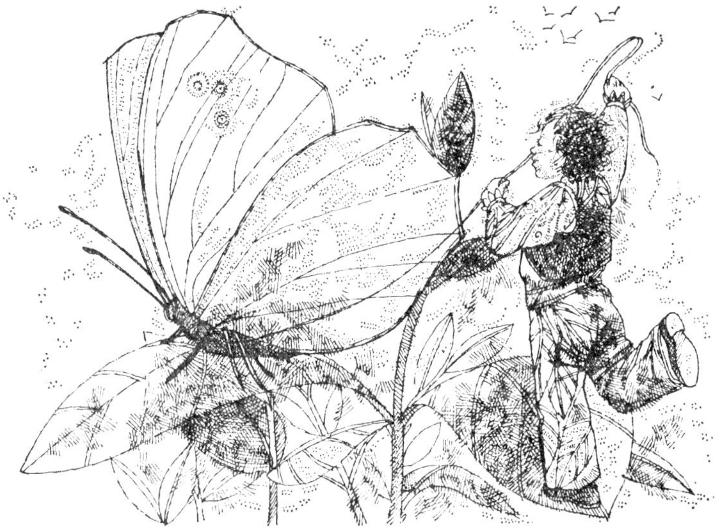

But all this time he had grown no bigger. He was still thumb-size, and it is very dangerous to be as small as that. It is also very dangerous to be favoured by a king. The queen was so jealous of the king's new friend that she was determined to put an end to him. So she told the king that the new knight had been rude to her.

The king sent for Tom at once, but Tom had already heard about the queen's anger and had crept into an empty snail shell to hide. He very nearly starved there, but then peeping out one day he saw a butterfly, jumped onto its back, and was carried into the air. The butterfly flew from tree to tree, and from field to field, and at last returned to court, where the king's courtiers managed to capture it, and so they caught Tom Thumb as well.

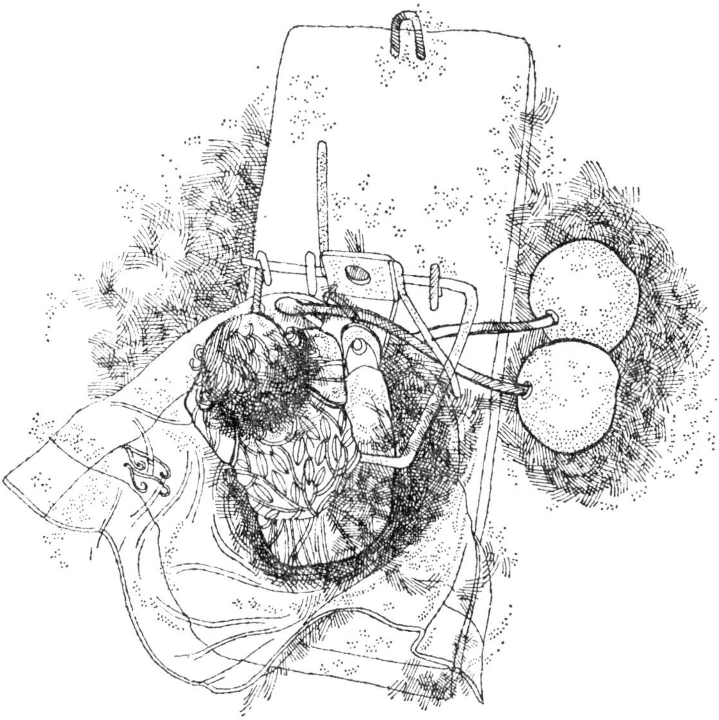

When the queen saw him she flew into a rage. She demanded that he be beheaded, and poor Tom was put into a mouse trap until the time of his execution.

But then a cat, seeing something alive in the trap, patted it about until the wires broke. Tom was free again, and at once went to the king to plead for his life.

The king pardoned him, and Tom lived very quietly for a long time, keeping out of sight and out of trouble.

Then one day he was attacked by a huge spider. Although he fought fiercely with his needle sword, the spider was too big for him and in the end he was killed.

The king and his court were very sad at the loss of their favourite. So that he should be remembered, they raised a fine white marble monument over his grave, and carved on it this verse:

Here lies Tom Thumb, King Arthur's knight,
Who died by a spider's cruel bite.
He was well known in Arthur's court,
Where he afforded gallant sport;
He rode at tilt and tournament,
And on a mouse a-hunting went.
Alive he filled the court with mirth;
His death to sorrow soon gave birth.
Oh wipe your eyes, and shake your head,
And cry, alas, Tom Thumb is dead!

The Sands of Ellenglaze

Over a thousand years ago, it is said, there was a city called Langarrow on the Cornish coast not far from Newquay. But one day a violent storm arose, and for three days and three nights, sand blew into the city. By the time the storm had subsided, the city was completely buried, and many of the inhabitants were dead.

Now nearby was a large house, the Hall of Ellenglaze, where the Lord of Ellenglaze lived. Although the house hadn't been damaged by the storm, the Lord's servants wanted him to move further inland where it might be safer. One of the servants was new, a young girl who'd arrived from Langarrow just before the storms had started, and she begged Lord Ellenglaze to listen to their advice. "What they say is right," she said. "The Hall of Ellenglaze stands in the path of the storms. If you stay here you will die, as the people of Langarrow have done."

The other servants were shocked to hear the girl speak so boldly to their master – she'd not been in his household a week! But Lord Ellenglaze took no notice of

her. He liked living in the house; it had belonged to his family for hundreds of years and he thought it unlikely that such a terrible storm could ever happen again. So, he ignored all the advice and decided to go on living at the Hall of Ellenglaze. But, soon the winds started to blow sand in from the coast again, and he began to wonder if the girl from Langarrow had been right, after all.

That night, as the wind howled round the house, Lord Ellenglaze called for more wine. The girl from Langarrow brought it and, as she poured it out, she whispered to him: "Master, wine may dull your fears but nothing can save your house."

Lord Ellenglaze's other servants were becoming more and more restless, and, when he asked what the matter was, the steward told him that the girl from Langarrow was going to leave the next morning. "Many of your servants want to go with her," he added. "She has frightened them with her talk of disaster to come."

Lord Ellenglaze was very angry – what right had the new girl to upset servants who'd been with him for many years? He demanded that she be brought before him.

"Leave my house," he shouted to the girl, "before your stir up any more trouble." Without a second thought, he had her turned out into the dark and stormy night.

But before the wind caught her up and carried her away, Lord Ellenglaze thought he saw the girl smile, and that it was the toothless smile of an old woman. The young servant-girl had grown suddenly old and, as she vanished into the night, the wind rose to a scream and the great door of Ellenglaze Hall slammed shut.

Lord Ellenglaze said nothing – it was so dark he knew he could have been mistaken. But one thing was certain, the storms that had buried the city of Langarrow had started again. The sand was lifted over the great sandhill and blown further and further inland. Soon it was too late to leave the house. If Lord Ellenglaze and his servants ventured outside the Hall, they would be

driven back by the raging winds and blinded by the flying sand. They were trapped.

After a night of storms and flying sand, the great house collapsed on top of Lord Ellenglaze and his servants. Like the city of Langarrow, Ellenglaze Hall was buried under a sandhill.

All that the new Lord Ellenglaze – a cousin of the first one – inherited, was a heap of sand. So he built a new house, much further inland, yet still in sight of the sea. But soon the storms that had destroyed Langarrow and the first Ellenglaze Hall started again. Sand was blown further and further inland, carried in on winds from the sea.

Soon the new house had so much sand banked against its walls it was in danger of collapsing. Just in time, Lord Ellenglaze and his servants escaped. As they fled, they saw an extraordinary thing. The house collapsed and the wind lifted the clouds of sand high into the air above the ruins. Those watching saw it spiralled, as if by a whirlwind, into the shape of an old woman. As the wind died down she vanished.

Lord Ellenglaze was puzzled by what had happened but, like his cousin, he was stubborn. He refused to be frightened when his servants insisted there was a curse on Ellenglaze, and that they'd seen the figure of a witch when his house fell down. Against all advice, he made plans to build a third Ellenglaze Hall. He had a special reason for building a new house and for making sure it would be safe. Lord Ellenglaze was in love, and was soon to marry a beautiful girl who lived some miles away.

So, after asking the advice of many learned men and hiring the best builders, he began to build his new house. He chose a sheltered spot where the sand from the coast had never settled, and had the walls built extra strong so that they would withstand any known storm. All around the house he planted trees as a windbreak. It was the grandest house that anyone in that part of Cornwall had seen. It was furnished with the finest things that money could buy, and marvellous tapestries hung on the wall. When at last the house seemed perfect, the wedding took place.

Lord Ellenglaze rode home with his beautiful young bride, and did not notice the storm clouds above his house – his only worry was that his bride should like the place he had built for her. But instead of being welcomed home, the young lord found that his servants were frightened. They whispered, and only smiled nervously when Lord Ellenglaze greeted them. "What's the trouble on this great day?" he asked his oldest servant.

"Master," he answered, "another storm is brewing and everyone is afraid. It's the same as before. The wind is blowing in from the sea . . . and sand is being carried far inland from the sandhills."

"But there can be nothing to fear," said Lord Ellenglaze calmly. "This house is strong enough to bear a mountain of sand. Come, let us not be so gloomy. Drink to the health of my Lady of Ellenglaze." A half-hearted cheer went up and wine was handed round. But clearly, the servants were frightened.

Lord Ellenglaze feared that his bride would be troubled by the gloominess of the servants, and ordered a feast to be prepared in her honour for the next night. Immediately, invitations were sent out to friends and neighbours. Musicians were engaged. The servants brought out silver goblets for the wine and golden platters for the food. And, although the storm was getting worse, there was so much excitement that gradually the servants forgot their fears. At last the guests began to arrive and were greeted by Lord and Lady Ellenglaze. When one of the guests said that there was an old woman sheltering from the wind in one of the stables, Lady Ellenglaze asked her husband if she could be brought in. "Of course, my dear," said Lord Ellenglaze, "she is welcome to join in our celebration."

The old woman was brought in to the house, and ate and drank at Lord Ellenglaze's table. But she never spoke, and nobody took much notice of her until after the feast, when the dancing began. Then the old woman leapt to her feet and danced so energetically that

many of the younger guests felt tired just watching her.

She whirled round and round like a spinning-top and, as he watched, Lord Ellenglaze remembered the figure he'd seen above the ruins of his first house.

The more the old woman danced, the worse the storm became. The house began to rattle and shake beneath its fury. The musicians tried playing louder, but soon they could not be heard above the noise of the wind.

So they stopped playing and everybody stopped dancing – everybody, that is, except the old woman. She seemed to be unable to stop. Suddenly one of the guests shouted: "Look, the sand! It's blocking up the windows."

Everyone was terrified. Women began to sob, and Lord Ellenglaze saw that his wife was weeping too. "There must be a curse on Ellenglaze after all," whispered the young lord. "But who has put it on my house?"

He looked round the room at the faces of his servants and of his guests. All of them seemed too frightened to move, exept for the old woman. She was still dancing.

"Stop! Stop at once!" commanded Lord Ellenglaze. He ran to the middle of the floor, caught the old woman and held her still. She wasn't out of breath and she wasn't crying. Her cold eyes stared at him, and made a shiver go up and down his spine.

Could it be she who'd put a curse on his family? Was she the figure he'd seen hovering over the ruins of his first house? Could she be a witch? She was the only woman who was not crying, and it was a known fact that witches never shed tears. "It's all your fault, you old hag," shouted Lord Ellenglaze. "Be off with you."

By now the storm had blown itself into a raging tempest and Lady Ellenglaze begged that the old woman should stay. "I'll not give shelter to a witch," retorted Lord Ellenglaze. "She shall go."

Lord Ellenglaze had a door forced open and the old woman was turned out into the storm. Lady Ellenglaze was so horrified at her husband's cruelty, she dashed out after her.

Lord Ellenglaze had made the same mistake as his cousin. When the old woman, disguised as a servant-girl, had been turned away from the first Ellenglaze Hall, she had put a curse on Lord Ellenglaze and all who succeeded to the title. Now there was no telling what she might do. Already the trees round the house had been uprooted by the storm, and the sand was blowing directly against the house.

In the storm, Lady Ellenglaze tried to catch up with the shadowy figure of the old woman. Both of them were carried along by the wind. "Dear old lady," she said as they reached the shelter of the stables, "I didn't want to send you away." And she leant forward and kissed her on the cheek.

The old woman was so startled by Lady Ellenglaze's kindness, she burst into tears.

"I knew you weren't a witch," exclaimed Lady Ellenglaze. "Witches don't cry."

"I was a witch," sobbed the old woman, "but now your kindness makes me ashamed of being so evil." As her tears fell on the ground, they formed a small stream. It flowed away between the house and the sandhills, running faster and faster until it reached the sea.

The storm died down and, at the same time, the stream widened into a river, across which the drifting sands couldn't pass. So, in breaking the spell of witchcraft, Lady Ellenglaze had also lifted the curse on her husband's family.

Today, the stream made by the old woman's tears still winds its way down to Holywell Bay near Newquay, protecting the village of Ellenglaze from the drifting sands.

Ainsel

A long time ago a small boy called Parcie lived with his mother in a stone cottage in the border country between England and Scotland. They were poor people and could afford only a table and two chairs and two beds, yet Parcie's mother managed to make it into a home-like place.

Every night a log fire burnt in the hearth, and Parcie and his mother would sit round it while she told him a story. And then every night when it was bedtime, his mother would say, "It's time you were away to your bed, Parcie."

Now, like many other boys and girls, Parcie made a great fuss when it was time for him to go to bed. He always said at least ten times that it was too early, but then as soon as he got into bed he fell asleep.

One night, however, Parcie's mother got very tired of listening to Parcie saying he wasn't going to bed. When he refused about six times to leave the fireside, she picked up the candle that lit the room and went off to bed herself, leaving Parcie alone by the fire.

Now in those days, there was a brownie who came down the chimney of each house and cottage every night to sweep the room and make everything clean and tidy.

Parcie's mother always left a bowl of goat's cream for their brownie as a way of thanking him for his work, and in the morning the bowl would be empty. For if any house forgot to leave a bowl of cream, then the brownie would turn the whole room topsy turvy and never go to that house again.

The brownie who came to help Parcie's mother always found his bowl of cream, and did his work quickly and quietly while everyone was asleep. But this brownie had a cross bad-tempered old faery mother.

Well, this particular night, Parcie stayed by the fire on his own after his mother had gone to bed, pleased that he had got his own way. After a time the fire began to lose its brightness and it became darker and colder. Parcie shivered, and was just about to go to bed after all, when he heard a noise in the chimney. Then down jumped the brownie. Parcie was as surprised to see the brownie as the brownie was to see Parcie. The brownie was very small – he just about came up to Parcie's knees – but he had long legs and funny pointed ears.

"What's your name?" asked Parcie.

"Ainsel," the brownie told him. "What's yours?"

Now Parcie knew the brownie was joking because Ainsel means one's own self, so he decided to be more clever, and told the brownie his name was My Ainsel – or "Myself."

Parcie and the brownie played together by the dying fire. After a while Parcie poked the fire to see if he could make it glow and become warm again, but all that happened was that a hot cinder fell out. And it fell on Ainsel's, the brownie's, foot. Ainsel yelled so loud that the old faery mother heard him and called down the chimney. "Tell me who's hurt you," she shouted, "and

I'll come down and whack him."

"It was *My* Ainsel," yelled the brownie up the chimney, standing on one leg and rubbing his foot. But it sounded as if it was he who had hurt himself.

"Weel, gin it was yourself who did it, what's all the fuss about? There's no name to blame but yourself." And a long, thin arm reached down the chimney and snatched up the brownie from the fireside. At this Parcie ran out of the door, jumped into bed and hid under the bedclothes. In the morning, Parcie's mother found the bowl still full of goat's cream.

The brownie never came to the cottage again. But although Parcie's mother had lost her faery helper, she was very pleased to find that Parcie always went to bed as soon as he was told. Because Parcie was afraid that if he stayed up late perhaps that long arm might be able to reach down the chimney and snatch his own self up and away!

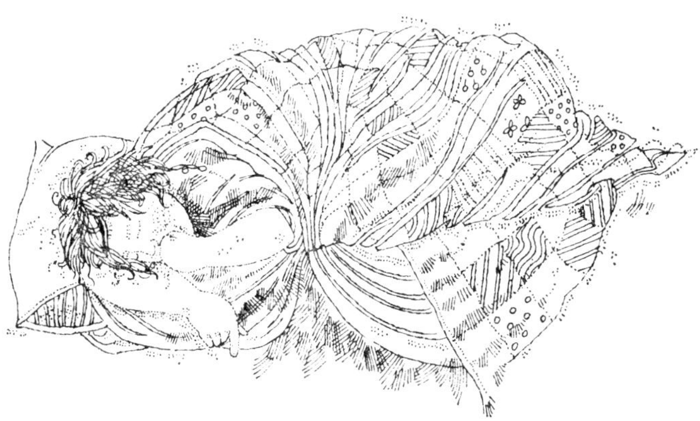

Mr and Mrs Vinegar

Mr and Mrs Vinegar lived in a vinegar bottle. It was made of brown glass. So whenever they looked out, everything looked brown. On one side there was a wooden door. Mrs. Vinegar kept their home spick and span – she was always polishing and dusting and sweeping it out with her broom. But one day she knocked the handle of her broom right through the side of the bottle and it broke into thousands of little pieces.

Mrs Vinegar stood among the ruins and cried and cried. "Oh dear, oh dear, whatever shall we do! Our home is gone. Our beautiful home!"

But Mr Vinegar looked about him cheerfully. "Never mind, my dear," he said. "Look how charming the world is! It isn't brown after all, you see my love. It's full of colour. The leaves are green and the sky is blue and – look, our door is all right!"

"Oh, what's the use of a door without a house behind it!" cried Mrs Vinegar. "You never know," said Mr Vinegar. "I'll carry it with us wherever we go."

So he put the door on his back. And he tucked Mrs

Vinegar's hand under his arm, and together they set off to seek their fortune.

All day long they trudged through the world, and as night fell they came to a deep dark forest.

"Oh, my goodness gracious!" cried Mrs Vinegar. "What a dreadful place. I'm sure there are wolves and snakes and monsters in it."

"There, there, my dear," said Mr Vinegar. "There probably are. But we'll lay our door across a branch, well out of reach of wolves and snakes and monsters – not that I think there are any really. And we'll sleep up there as cosy as anything, my love. You'll see."

So that's what they did. And Mrs Vinegar dried her eyes and lay down beside her husband and soon they were fast asleep.

But in the middle of the night when it was quite dark, they both woke up with a start. There were voices below – rough, growling voices.

"My share's ten guineas," said one.

"So's mine," said another.

"Twenty for Peg-leg Pete."

"Count it out! Fair now!"

"Is it robbers?" asked Mrs Vinegar.

"Yes, my love. Keep very still," whispered Mr Vinegar. But Mrs Vinegar was so frightened she didn't keep still at all. She began to shake, and as she shook the door shook – till suddenly it fell right on top of the robbers!

They didn't know what had hit them, so they all ran away as fast as they could. Mr and Mrs Vinegar stayed up in the tree till sunrise and then, when they saw that it was quite safe, they crept down and lifted up their door.

And underneath, there was a pile of golden guineas. Mrs Vinegar could hardly believe her eyes. "Didn't I tell you all was for the best when we lost our home?" cried Mr Vinegar. "We are rich. Rich as kings, my love!" And he danced a little dance among the tree-trunks.

"That's all very well," called Mrs Vinegar. "But what shall we spend it on?"

"Oh, I know just the thing," said Mr Vinegar. "Give me the money and I'll go and buy it right away."

"You will be careful, won't you?" called Mrs Vinegar.

"Of course I will. Don't worry, my love," laughed Mr Vinegar. And off he went whistling.

He hadn't gone very far when he met a farmer on the road. He was driving a big red cow to market.

"That's just what I want," thought Mr Vinegar. "A fine red cow to give us milk and butter and cheese for breakfast. And I dare say she'll give us eggs too if we ask her nicely!" Then he asked: "Will you sell that cow to me?"

"It depends on how much money you've got," said the farmer sharply.

"Oh I've got forty guineas," said Mr Vinegar.

"Then that's what this cow costs," said the farmer. And he held out his hand. Well, forty guineas would have bought seven cows in those days. But Mr Vinegar was so pleased with his one cow that he didn't stop to think. And as soon as the farmer had gone, he took off his hat and sat down to milk her.

But the cow didn't like Mr Vinegar one bit! She walked a little way to the left. Then she walked a little way to the right. And all of a sudden she kicked Mr Vinegar's hat clean over the fence.

Then she galloped off down the road in the opposite direction. Mr Vinegar chased after her. And they were

still running when they heard the sound of pipes far ahead.

Coming towards them was a piper, and behind him followed a crowd of laughing children. As he played they threw pennies into his pockets and his pockets were already bulging.

When he saw Mr Vinegar, the piper stopped playing. "That's a fine cow you've got there," he said.

"Oh, I don't know about that," said Mr Vinegar. "I'd much rather have those pipes you're playing. I'd change this old cow for those pipes any day!"

"Would you really?" said the piper.

"Yes, I would," said Mr Vinegar.

"Right you are then," said the piper. "That's a bargain."

So Mr Vinegar took the pipes. And catching hold of the cow by its horns the piper marched off down the road and was soon out of sight.

"Oh what a lucky man I am!" laughed Mr Vinegar, and he gathered all the children around him. "Listen, my little chickabiddies," said he, "I'll play you a tune to set your feet a-dancing."

But oh dear, when Mr Vinegar tried to play them, the noise the pipes made was terrible. The children covered up their ears and ran away as fast as they could. Mr Vinegar was left all alone in the road trying to play the pipes.

It was a cold day, and it wasn't long before his hands turned blue.

Just then a man came along the road, and he was wearing a fine thick pair of gloves.

"Oh," said Mr Vinegar, "my fingers are so very cold. If only I had that pair of gloves I should be the happiest man alive."

When he saw Mr Vinegar, the man said: "My, that's a fine pair of pipes you have there!"

"Oh, I don't know about that," said Mr Vinegar. "I'd much rather have those fine thick gloves you're wearing."

"Would you really?" asked the man.

"Yes, I would," said Mr Vinegar.

"Right you are then," said the man. "That's a bargain."

So Mr Vinegar put on the gloves while the man went off with the pipes. He played them every bit as well as the Piper.

Well, Mr Vinegar was still a long way from home. He walked and he walked and he walked. And just when he thought he couldn't take another step he was so tired, he saw an old lady coming through the wood towards him. She was leaning on a thick white stick.

Mr Vinegar thought how much he'd like that stick for his own tired feet. So he said to her: "Good morning to you, Ma'am. I see you have no gloves on your hands, and I, as you see, have no stick to help me walk. I wonder whether you would mind changing one for the other?"

"Why certainly," said the old lady – for she knew

sticks were easy to come by. She put them on and went on her way quickly before Mr Vinegar could change his mind.

All of a sudden, Mr Vinegar saw where he was. Right back where he'd started! Round the very next clump of trees was Mrs Vinegar, still sitting on the door at the bottom of the tree where they'd spent the night.

"Well," she said when she saw Mr Vinegar, "what have you bought with the forty guineas?"

Mr Vinegar held up the stick. And for the first time in his life, he didn't feel so cheerful.

"What?" cried Mrs Vinegar. "Is that all you got – just a stick? You have nothing more to show for our forty guineas than a miserable stick you could cut from any hedge?" Snatching the stick from his hand, she began to beat her husband, chasing him round the tree trunks until they were both exhausted. "There! That's what I think about your silly old stick!" sobbed Mrs Vinegar, and she threw it high up in the air. As it came down to earth again, they heard a strange whistling sound behind them.

"What was that?" asked Mr Vinegar.

"I don't know," said Mrs Vinegar, "and I don't care."

"All the same, I think we'd better see, my love," said Mr Vinegar.

So they did.

And what should they find but a new vinegar bottle! It was just the same as their old one except that it had no door.

Mr Vinegar fetched their old door and fixed it in. And Mrs Vinegar made herself a new broom out of soft twigs, so that there would be less risk of damage in the future.

"I told you everything would work out for the best in the end, didn't I my love?' said Mr Vinegar.

Mrs Vinegar said nothing, but for once she seemed to have a smile on her face instead of a frown.

Tam Lin

Long, long ago in the border country lived a very beautiful girl. She was known to everybody as Fair Janet.

Her father was a rich earl and they lived in a splendid castle surrounded by rolling hills and green meadows.

Now, even though Janet had everything anyone could wish for – good looks, a loving family and beautiful clothes, she was often bored.

One day when she was feeling particularly bored, she plaited her long yellow hair, threw a cloak around her shoulders and set off to explore the woods of Carterhaugh nearby. It was a sunny day and she wandered for several hours along the woodland paths. For once she felt happy and contented. All around her grew wild briers, still full of roses in the most lovely shades of red and pink. Suddenly Janet saw a bush of white roses. They were bigger than any other roses Janet had ever seen and their perfume was sweeter than anything Janet had ever smelt before. She bent down

and plucked one. But just as she did so, a young man suddenly stepped onto the path in front of her. He was furious. "How dare you pluck the roses of Carterhaugh without my permission!" he exclaimed.

Janet was so startled that she dropped the white rose. "I'm sorry, I meant no harm," she answered.

The young man, no longer angry, explained that it was his job to guard the woods and to make sure no one disturbed their peace. "But," he went on, "I would gladly give all the roses of Carterhaugh to one as lovely as you." Then he smiled slowly and picked up from the path the white rose that Janet had dropped, and plucked two more from the bush.

"Who are you?" asked Janet, taking the roses he offered her.

"My name is Tam Lin," the young man replied.

"Tam Lin! I have heard of you – you are an elfin knight," cried Janet.

Tam Lin sat down on a grassy bank. "Do not be afraid of me," he said. "Although I am called an elfin knight, I was born a mortal child just as you were yourself. Come, sit down here with me and I will tell you my story."

Janet sat down on the bank by him and Tam Lin began. "My father and mother died when I was but a child, and my grandfather, the Earl of Roxburgh, took me to live with him. He was very kind and looked after me very well. And he taught me to hunt and do all the things a young nobleman should do. One day we went hunting in these very woods. Suddenly I felt a strange cold wind blow. I could no longer keep my eyes open and I wanted only to sleep. I must have lagged further and further behind my companions until at last I did fall asleep. When I woke up, I found myself in Faeryland, standing before the Elf Queen herself – for it was she who had stolen me away as I slept."

Tam Lin paused as he thought of the Faeryland where he had lived for so long. Then he went on with his story: "Ever since the day I was taken to Faeryland I have been bound fast by the spell the Elf Queen put on me. In the daytime, I have to guard the woods of Carterhaugh, and at night I must return to Faeryland."

Tam Lin paused again for a moment and looked hard at Janet. Then he went on: "With all my heart I wish I could break the Elf Queen's spell and return to the land of the mortals."

He sounded so sad that Janet cried out, "But is there no way this can be done?"

Tam Lin took her hands in his. "Tonight is Halloween," he said, "and on this night of all nights, there is a chance to win me back to mortal life. But it will be dangerous."

"Just tell me what I must do," said Janet, "and it

shall be done – for I *do* want to help you."

"Thank you," said Tam Lin. "Tonight, at midnight, you must go to the cross-roads and wait for the Elf Queen and her court to come past. As the first company approaches you, stay still and let them pass. And as the second company draws near let them pass also. But I shall be among the third company, riding a milk-white steed and wearing a gold circlet on my brow. Then you must run to me and throw your arms tight around me. And no matter what spells the Elf Queen may cast, you must hold me as tight as you can and do not let me go. This is the only way the spell may be broken."

Janet promised to do exactly as Tam Lin had told her. Then she left him and went home to her castle.

That night Janet went to bed but not to sleep.

Just before midnight she dressed quickly, and crept out of the castle making sure no one heard or saw her.

She reached the crossroads as the clock struck midnight, and hid behind a thorn bush. The moon cast strange shadows on the ground and the wind whistled and rustled the branches of the trees above her. Janet shivered a little and drew her cloak round her. As she peered ahead of her into the darkness she heard a sound and saw the Elf Queen and her courtiers approaching.

Soon the road was full of fairy horses. As the first company passed her, with the Elf Queen herself mounted on a black horse, Janet stayed as still as she could just as she had been told.

The company passed by without knowing Janet was

there. Nor did she move when the second company went by. But among the third company she saw the milk-white horse that carried Tam Lin, and she saw the moonlight reflected in the gold circlet on his head.

She jumped up from behind her thorn bush and ran to the horse. She seized the bridle, and pulled Tam Lin down onto the ground where she clasped him in her arms. The Elf Queen reined her black horse to a halt and galloped back to where Janet lay on the ground still clasping Tam Lin to her.

The Elf Queen waved her hands through the air and whispered mysterious words. She had cast a spell on Tam Lin, so that he shrank smaller and smaller in Janet's grasp and then changed into a green scaly lizard. But Janet remembered what Tam Lin had told her about holding on tight to him no matter what happened, and clutched the lizard tight to her heart.

The Elf Queen began waving her hands in the air once again, and whispered more mysterious words. She was casting yet another spell.

Janet felt a slithering through her fingers and the lizard changed into a cold slippery snake. But still Janet held onto it, even though it hissed and coiled itself around her neck.

The Elf Queen passed her hands through the air yet again whispering more mysterious words and the snake turned into a red-hot bar of iron. Tears ran down Janet's cheeks as she felt the iron burning into her skin. But she held on tight.

At this the Elf Queen could see that she had been beaten at last. Her spell had been broken by the true love of a mortal woman, and there was nothing she could do. Then the red hot iron changed into a mortal man. It was Tam Lin as he had been on the day the Elf Queen had spirited him away from his grandfather's hunting party. As the Elf Queen's court rode away, the queen turned to Tam Lin and Janet.

"Farewell, Tam Lin!" she cried. "The bonniest knight in my company is lost again to the world of mortals. If I had known that an earthly woman would win you with her love, I would have taken out your heart of flesh and put in a heart of stone. Farewell!"

As she galloped away, a faint dawn light came to the forest and the Elf Queen and her court vanished – leaving only the sound of their bridle bells.

Tam Lin turned to Fair Janet and kissed her hands, blistered from holding the red-hot iron bar. "By your love you have saved me and brought me back to the world of mortals," he said. "Now will you be my wife?"

"I will, and gladly," replied Janet. Then the two of them walked hand in hand through the forest towards her father's castle.

Cap of Rushes

There was once a rich gentleman who lived in a castle with a lot of fine lands. He had three daughters, and he loved them all, but the youngest daughter was most dear to him. He did all he could to please her, and he had given her three grand dresses. One was of silver cloth, the second was of beaten gold, and the third was made of the feathers of all the birds of the air.

One day the man called his three daughters together and he asked the first: "Daughter, how much do you love me?"

And the first daughter answered straight away, "As much as I love my life."

"That's good," said he.

Then he asked the second daughter: "Daughter, how much do you love me?"

And the second daughter answered straight away, "Better than all the world."

"That's good," said he.

So he asked the youngest daughter, "Daughter, how much do you love me?"

And she thought how she should answer him, and then she said: "I love you as much as meat loves salt."

Now her father wasn't at all pleased with this reply. "You don't love me at all," he said, angrily. "Leave my house! I never want to see you again."

The poor girl, feeling very sad that she couldn't please her father, whom she loved very much, packed up her three fine dresses in a big trunk. The one of silver cloth, the one of beaten gold, and the one made of feathers of all the birds of the air. And saying goodbye to her sisters, she left her father's house forever.

Well, she went along and she went along and she went along until she came to a fen – and there she began to pick rushes. She picked until she had enough to weave them into a cloak with a hood, which covered her from head to foot, and hid her fine clothes. And she buried the trunk with her three dresses in a cave by a stream.

Then she went on her way until she came to a great house where she asked if she could be a maid, or cook, or work in the kitchen. "I haven't anywhere to go," she said, "and I ask for no wages. I'll do any sort of work if you'll let me stay."

"Well, if you'll wash the pots and scrape the saucepans and be a scullion you may stay," said the cook.

So the girl stayed in the kitchen, doing all the dirty

work, and because she told no one her name they called her Cap of Rushes.

Now one day, it so happened that the young lord of the house was coming home and there was to be a grand ball for the occasion. All the servants were allowed to go and look at the people arriving. But Cap of Rushes said she was too tired to go, so she stayed in the kitchen.

As soon as she was alone she went off to the cave by the stream where she had hidden her trunk, took off her cloak of rushes, and washed herself in the sparkling water. Then, putting on her fine dress of silver cloth, off she went to the ball.

As soon as the young lord saw her, he fell in love with her and would dance with no one else.

But before the dance was done, Cap of Rushes slipped off and went away back to her kitchen. When the other maids came back, there she was, in her cloak of rushes, pretending to be asleep.

"You did miss a sight, Cap o' Rushes. The most beautiful lady you ever did see, dressed right gay and grand in a dress all of silver cloth and the young master never took his eyes off her!"

"Oh! I would like to have seen her!" said Cap of Rushes.

"Well, there's to be another dance this evening, and perhaps she'll be there."

When evening came, Cap of Rushes again said she

was too tired to go with the others. But as soon as they had gone, she ran to the cave, having washed herself in the stream, put on her dress of beaten gold, and went off to the ball.

As soon as she entered all eyes were upon her, and the young lord, recognising her as the lady he had danced with before, claimed her hand for the first dance – and danced with no one else.

But before the dance was over she slipped away to her hiding place, took off her golden dress and put on her cap of rushes. And when the maids came back, there she was in the kitchen pretending to be asleep.

The next day they said to her again, "Well, Cap o' Rushes, you should have been there last night. She was there again – gay and grand in a dress of beaten gold, and the young lord he never took his eyes off her."

And Cap of Rushes said, "There, I would have liked to have seen that."

"Well, there's a dance again this evening," they said. "And this time you must go with us, for she's sure to be there."

But when evening came, Cap of Rushes said she was too tired to go, and however much they asked her she said she would not go.

As soon as she was alone, as before, she ran off to the cave by the stream, bathed in the water and put

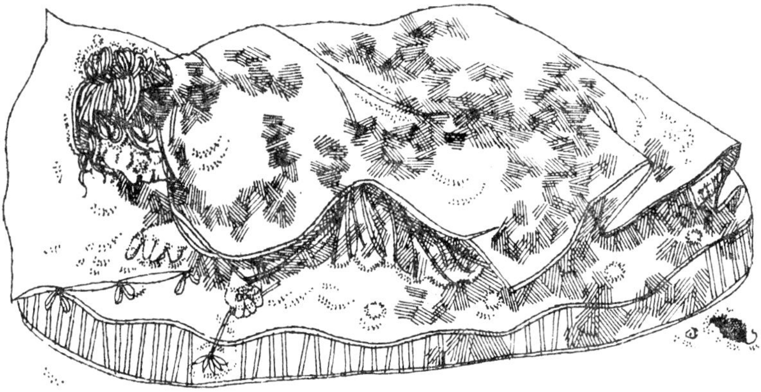

on her third dress – the one made of the feathers of all the birds of the air.

Everyone was surprised to see so beautiful a face and form dressed in so rich and rare a dress, and the young lord recognised his sweetheart and would dance with none but her.

While they danced he said, "Pray, tell me fair maid, what is your name and where do you live?" But she would not tell him, so he gave her a ring and told her that if he did not see her again he would surely die.

Before the dance was over off she slipped and home she went. And when the maids came back she was pretending to be asleep with her cap of rushes on just as before. Next day they said to her: "There, Cap o' Rushes, you didn't come last night, and now you won't ever see the lady, for there's to be no more dances."

"Oh," said Cap of Rushes, "I should like to have seen her."

The young lord tried every way he could to find out where the lady had gone, but go where he might, and ask whom he might, he never heard anything of her. He was so grieved that he took to his bed and grew paler and paler and fell ill for love of her. "Make some broth for the young lord," they said to the cook. "He's dying for the love of the lady."

So the cook set about making some broth, when Cap of Rushes came in. "What are you doing?" she asked.

"I'm making some broth for the young lord," said the cook, "for he's dying for love of the lady."

"Let me do it," begged Cap of Rushes. At first the cook wouldn't let her, but at last she said "yes," and Cap of Rushes made the broth. And, before the cook took it upstairs, she slipped the ring the young lord had given her into the bowl. The young man drank the broth and then saw the ring at the bottom.

"Send for the cook!" he shouted.

So up came the cook.

"Who made this broth?" he asked.

"I did," said the cook, for she was frightened.

"No you didn't," said he. "Say who did, and you shan't be harmed."

"Well, then, it was Cap o' Rushes," she said.

"Send Cap o' Rushes here."

So Cap of Rushes came.

"Did you make my broth?" asked he.

"Yes, I did, young master."

"And where did you get this ring?"

"From him who gave it me," said she. And she took off her cloak of rushes and there she stood in her beautiful dress of feathers.

The young lord soon got well and in a little time they were to be married. It was to be a very grand wedding and everyone was asked from near and far. And Cap of Rushes's father was asked too. But she never told anyone who she was.

Before the wedding, Cap of Rushes went to the cook and said: "I want you to make every dish of meat for the wedding feast without even a wee bit of salt in it."

"That'll taste rare nasty," said the cook.

"That doesn't matter. Do as I ask," said she.

"Very well," said the cook.

So the wedding day came and they were married. And afterwards the whole company sat down to the wedding feast. But when they began to try the meat, it was so tasteless they couldn't eat it.

Cap of Rushes's father tried one dish and then another and then another, and then he burst out crying.

"Why are you crying, old man?" asked the young lord.

"Once I had a daughter," said he, and I asked her how much she loved me, and she said, 'As much as meat loves salt.' And I turned her away from my house for I thought she didn't love me. And now, I can see that she loved me best of all. She may be dead for all I know. I would give all my worldy goods to hold her in my arms once more."

"Father, father, here I am," said Cap of Rushes, and she rushed up to him and put her arms round him. And the great wedding feast went on and on, and they all lived happily ever after.

The Lost Land of Lyonesse

Long, long ago, it is said, there was land beyond Cornwall. Where the Atlantic ocean now surges beyond Land's End, was Lyonesse, a rich and fertile land with farms and villages, grand palaces and churches. And the bells of Lyonesse, ringing out from church steeples, could be heard throughout Cornwall.

Lyonesse was there when King Arthur held his court at Tintagel. There his knights assembled, but when this story begins, towards the end of Arthur's reign, there were many empty seats at the Round Table.

One night at a banquet, the King sadly looked around the table and remembered those many knights who had been killed in his service. Even his friend Merlin the Wizard, whose magic had helped him so often, was dead. Then King Arthur's eyes rested on one place in particular – the empty chair of Prince Mordred, his cousin, who had disappeared from court.

It was rumoured that Mordred had evil plans against King Arthur – even so far as to declare open war on him – because Mordred wanted to be king. But Arthur

and his knights paid little heed to these rumours.

When everyone at the table had eaten their fill, King Arthur took a golden cup in his hands and rose to his feet to drink the health of his guests. The company watched as he raised the cup to his lips. He tasted the wine and shuddered.

The noise and laughter died down as the King spoke: "This is not wine but blood," he exclaimed in horror. "Merlin has sent this as a sign that there is evil in the coming days. Break up our court, my friends, this is no time for feasting."

As he left the hall, he glanced at the empty seat of his cousin Mordred, and thought he saw a shadowy figure there. It had no real shape, it seemed like a cloud

that rested in Mordred's place, and then disappeared. An icy wind seemed to fill the hall, and the knights dispersed, sure that something terrible was about to happen.

The very next morning, a messenger arrived at Tintagel with the news the Prince Mordred had gathered an army to fight against Arthur's knights – the few that were left.

The king ordered his men to stay hidden inside the castle, and wait for his signal to attack, while he and his look-outs kept watch.

At last, he saw Mordred's army silently creeping up on the castle. As he watched them advance, Arthur thought of the times that he and his cousin had ridden

into battle side by side, under the same flag. Mordred came nearer and nearer, but Arthur gave no sign to his men to attack until the enemy was almost at the gates of the castle. Then he gave the signal, the great bell of Tintagel castle rang out, and King Arthur rode through the gates, followed by his knights.

They were hopelessly outnumbered. But Arthur and his men were no cowards, and rode out boldly.

When Arthur came face to face with Mordred, he stopped. "Cousin," he said, "this is an evil day." But Mordred made no reply, and signalled to his men to commence battle.

Spears and lances cut through the air and, though the knights of the Round Table fought bravely, many fell, and soon only the king and a handful of his knights were left.

Then a lance struck King Arthur from his horse. His knights rode to his aid, but the lance had pierced his heart. The great King Arthur was dead. His knights had no heart to fight on, so they covered his body with his banner and bore him from the battlefield.

But instead of seeking the safety of Tintagel, they tied Arthur's body to his horse and rode westwards. They were heading for the land of Lyonesse which stretched out into the Atlantic Ocean. In the hills to the west were the graves of great heroes, and the knights of the Round Table wanted their king to buried with them. So, tired and defeated, they bore him westwards.

Sometimes they stopped at a stream or brook for their horses to drink, and then rode slowly on. Some even dropped off their horses from sheer exhaustion.

Yet Mordred's victory was an uneasy one. He couldn't become king until all who opposed him were dead. For if even one of Arthur's knights remained alive, he might raise an army against him.

Mordred decided to ride after the knights, keeping out of sight until they reached the western coast of Lyonesse, and then to charge at them and drive them into the sea. They wouldn't stand a chance against his massive army, and even Merlin's magic couldn't save them from drowning.

Arthur's men rode more and more slowly as evening came, but still Mordred and his followers kept out of sight, waiting until Arthur's men were far ahead of them before riding on again.

By the time it got dark, they had ridden over thirty miles of rough and broken roads, and decided to call a halt. They prepared a camp for the night, but they were not able to rest for long. Shortly before day-break they heard the sound of horses riding towards them. It was Mordred's army, closing in on them!

Arthur's weary men mounted their horses again and fled towards Land's End, Mordred on their heels. They were lost without their leader, and ashamed that they, the most admired knights in the land, were fleeing for their lives from the traitor Mordred.

Suddenly, a trumpet was heard. Then it came louder and louder still. Too late, they saw the air was bright with the glint of sunlight on steel shields and lances on the brow of a nearby hill.

Mordred's men had almost caught up with them. Should they make a stand against them – and die? Or ride westwards and be chased into the sea?

They paused, and as they watched, a rolling mist gathered round Mordred's men. It was like a mountain mist – but then it formed itself into the shape of Merlin – who had helped their king many times before and was helping them now by turning into a mist. It separated

Mordred's men from Arthur's.

So, even after King Arthur's death, Merlin still watched over his men. The mist was so thick that none of Mordred's men could see where they were riding.

Now one of Arthur's knights had been severely wounded and could go no further. He managed to reach a hut where a lonely hermit lived. The knight was dying, and the hermit gave him shelter and knelt by him and prayed. But there was nothing the hermit could do to save him, and he died. As the hermit prayed, hooves

were heard outside, and up rode Mordred.

He recognised the dead knight. Once, when Mordred had fought on Arthur's side, this knight had been one of his closest friends. For a moment he was sad – but his sadness soon turned to anger when the old hermit rose from his prayers and spoke: "In one day you have done more evil than all your ancestors in the whole of their lives," he said. "Go, you traitor to God and man!" Mordred was so angry, he struck the old man with his hand.

“Go on,” said the hermit, “your journey is done. The shadow of Merlin is over you. Go on – and die.”

The hermit’s words were soon to come true. As Mordred turned his horse to ride away, a dark cloud formed in the sky above the sea to the north, and followed him. Mordred didn’t see the cloud and, as he urged his men forward, it became tinged with red.

Mordred rode ahead and then spurred his horse up a high slope. From there he could see his enemies riding slowly along the winding road that joined Cornwall to the Isles of Scilly. Now was the time to chase after them and drive them westwards into the sea. He urged his horse forward, but the animal refused to obey. Only when he dug his spurs into its side did it move, and it seemed to Mordred that he was riding against an unknown force, something that terrified his horse.

However hard Mordred and his men tried, they could not catch up with Arthur’s knights. They chased them through the Land of Lyonesse, and, just as Arthur’s men reached the hills to the west of the country, Mordred’s horse stopped and would not move.

Mordred's men drew close round him and, now terrified, watched a shape forming from the cloud that had followed them. It was Merlin again. Slowly, slowly, Merlin raised his arm, and as he did so the sea rose into a gigantic wave. It loomed over Mordred and his knights for a few brief seconds – and before they could move it crashed down on them.

Mordred and his soldiers were whirled away in the water – powerless against the great wave. Where, that morning, land had been, was nothing but a howling and boiling wilderness of waves.

Arthur's men reached the safety of the hills which now stood as islands surrounded by the sea.

No one knows where King Arthur's grave is, but he was supposed to have been buried on one of those islands. His men never returned to the mainland, for without their king it would be a changed and sad place. The knights of the Round Table were gone for ever. But those that came to the islands lived peacefully and died there – and then were forgotten.

But people still say that, if you listen, you can sometimes hear the bells of the Lost Land of Lyonesse, tolling out beneath the sea.